What-If Science?

Could We Bring Dinosaurs Back to Life?

Cynthia O'Brien

Lerner Publications ◆ Minneapolis

Lerner Publications Company
An imprint of Lerner Publishing Group, Inc.
241 First Avenue North
Minneapolis, MN 55401 USA

For reading levels and more information, look up this title at www.lernerbooks.com.

Main body text set in Adrianna Regular.
Typeface provided by Chank.

Library of Congress Cataloging-in-Publication Data

Names: O'Brien, Cynthia (Cynthia J.) author
Title: Could we bring dinosaurs back to life? / Cynthia O'Brien.
Description: Minneapolis : Lerner Publications, [2026] | Series: What-if science? | Includes bibliographical references and index. | Audience: Ages 8–11 | Audience: Grades 4–6 | Summary: "To bring dinosaurs back to life, we need to find their DNA. We have only ever found fossils and bones. Discover what is required to create a dinosaur today, and how it might work"—Provided by publisher.
Identifiers: LCCN 2025011286 (print) | LCCN 2025011287 (ebook) | ISBN 9798765688984 library binding | ISBN 9798348029180 paperback | ISBN 9798765698143 epub
Subjects: LCSH: Dinosaurs—Cloning—Juvenile literature | Dinosaurs—Extinction—Juvenile literature | Dinosaurs—Genetic engineering—Juvenile literature | DNA, Fossil—Juvenile literature
Classification: LCC QE861.5 .O266 2026 (print) | LCC QE861.5 (ebook) | DDC 567.9—dc23/eng/20250721

LC record available at https://lccn.loc.gov/2025011286
LC ebook record available at https://lccn.loc.gov/2025011287

Manufactured in the United States of America
1 – CG – 12/15/25

Table of Contents

Chapter 1

FROZEN IN TIME

In 2022 scientists uncovered an amazing secret. They found tiny samples of DNA in northern Greenland. The samples were from animals and plants. Greenland is an island in the North Atlantic Ocean that is covered in ice and snow. Frozen clay had preserved the DNA. The samples were two million years old. This is the oldest DNA ever found.

The DNA revealed a surprise. It proved that mastodons once lived on Greenland. American mastodons were animals similar to elephants that have been extinct for about thirteen thousand years. Before 2022 mastodon fossils had only been found in warmer forests in North America. The DNA also showed that Greenland was much warmer millions of years ago. It showed that the island was covered in trees and plants when mastodons lived there.

Greenland's icy conditions preserved ancient DNA samples.

The Key to Dinosaur Life

The discovery in Greenland led to exciting questions. Could scientists find dinosaur DNA, which is much older than mastodon DNA? Should they look in other frozen places where DNA could be preserved? If they found dinosaur DNA, could they use it to bring dinosaurs back to life?

SCIENTISTS STUDY DINOSAUR BONES TO FIND OUT HOW THESE ANIMALS LIVED.

Deep Dive

What is DNA?

DNA is in the cells of every living thing. It holds the instructions for how people, animals, and plants look and function. The structure of DNA is different for everyone. DNA makes copies of itself when new cells form. Over time, DNA is damaged and lost. After an animal or plant dies, DNA starts to break down right away. It is rare that parts of it get preserved like the mastodon DNA.

DNA is shaped like a twisted ladder.

Fact or Fiction?

There are many movies, TV shows, and books about dinosaurs coming back to life. In some stories, people discover that dinosaurs never died out. In other stories, scientists use bones or preserved DNA to bring dinosaurs back from extinction. These are fictional, or made-up, stories.

Dinosaur models are popular attractions in museums and galleries.

In real life scientists are still looking for clues to bring back prehistoric life. Some clues have been preserved in amber fossils. Amber is a hardened tree resin that takes more than forty thousand years to form. Scientists have found insects, flowers, and feathers preserved in amber. It also preserves bits of skin and cells. Dinosaur fossils are mainly found in rock. These fossils are so old that they have not preserved cells or whole DNA. Unless scientists find cells or DNA, bringing dinosaurs back to life is impossible.

Small creatures get stuck in sticky tree resin, which hardens to make amber.

Chapter 2

GOING, GOING, GONE

Earth is about 4.5 billion years old. Life began about 3.7 billion years ago, but it did not include animals as we know them today. The first life on Earth was made up of tiny, simple organisms. The first animals were sponges that lived in the oceans. They appeared about 890 million years ago. More and more kinds of animals evolved.

Then, about 440 million years ago, all the small sea organisms died out. This was the first mass, or large, extinction on Earth.

Four other mass extinctions followed. They were caused by natural changes on Earth, such as extreme changes in temperature. One of these extinctions, more than 250 million years ago, wiped out most life on Earth. This made way for the dinosaurs.

Sea sponges were the first animals on Earth.

The stegosaurus lived about 150 million years ago.

The Age of Dinosaurs

Dinosaurs ruled Earth for more than 150 million years. Scientists divide this time into three main periods. The Triassic is the earliest, the Jurassic is in the middle, and the Cretaceous is the last. Different types of dinosaurs lived during each of these periods. They also died out at different times. The massive Camarasaurus lived during the Jurassic period. So did the stegosaurus.

Both dinosaurs were already extinct when the Tyrannosaurus rex and Hadrosaurus were alive. These and other late Cretaceous dinosaurs died out last. This fifth mass extinction happened sixty-six million years ago. All the non-avian dinosaurs and many plants and other animals died out. The birdlike dinosaurs survived and evolved into today's birds.

The Tyrannosaurus rex was a powerful hunter, with teeth up to 8 inches (20 cm) long.

What Happened?

Scientists are not sure why most dinosaurs became extinct. One possible reason is that a massive asteroid struck Earth. Asteroids are space objects made of rock and metal that circle the sun. Scientists think that a large, heavy asteroid—measuring 6 to 9 miles (10 to 16 km) across—hit Earth at great speed. It made a huge, deep crater. Evidence of this massive crater has been found in Mexico.

This bowl-shaped crater was made when a meteor hit Earth.

The impact of the asteroid killed about 75 percent of Earth's animals.

Some dinosaurs may have been killed by the asteroid right away. Others died out over time. An asteroid hitting Earth would have created a dense cloud of dust and rock. The dust cloud around Earth probably blocked the sun for years. This would have killed the plants and choked other animals. Dinosaurs would have had nothing to eat.

The People Problem

Natural events caused the dinosaurs and other prehistoric animals to disappear. Today, Earth is a very different place from the one that dinosaurs left. If dinosaurs came back, could they survive on today's planet?

Humans have destroyed forests to make way for roads and farmland.

People have built cities and taken over animal habitats. They have polluted the oceans and the air. This has caused many modern animals to become extinct. Animals such as the passenger pigeon and Steller's sea cow have disappeared. Many other animals and plants are endangered. This means that they are at risk of becoming extinct.

The last passenger pigeon died in 1914.

Chapter 3

BACK TO LIFE

Paleontologists are scientists who study fossils. They discover new fossils all the time. Fossils reveal a lot about extinct animals and plants. Scientists can figure out how animals looked, what they ate, and what their habitats looked like. In 2024 paleontologists finished putting together fossils found in 2019.

Scientists named the new dinosaur *Lokiceratops rangiformis*. This horned dinosaur lived in the late Cretaceous period. In the future, a new discovery may hold enough DNA for scientists to reconstruct whole dinosaur DNA.

***Lokiceratops rangiformis* had a heavy body and large horns.**

De-extinction is bringing extinct animals and plants back to life. Scientists have already done this. In 2000 the last Pyrenean ibex died. An ibex is a type of wild goat. A year before the ibex died, scientists took some of its cells. In 2009 the scientists implanted ibex DNA into fifty-seven female goats.

One of the goats had a baby ibex, but it only lived for a few minutes. Though the ibex did not survive, scientists are trying to bring back other extinct animals. These include the Tasmanian tiger and the dodo, an extinct bird.

Dodos were flightless birds that lived on the island of Mauritius.

Deep Dive

Finding Ancient DNA

Scientists extract, or remove, DNA in a lab. They start with a small sample of body tissue, such as bone. Next, they break open the cells. Then DNA is separated using special formulas and a spinning machine called a centrifuge. The collected DNA must be cleaned and then copied. This is much more difficult to do with DNA that is damaged or broken down.

A scientist puts tissue samples into a centrifuge.

Changing Over Time

Most birds, such as small robins and chickadees, do not look anything like their dinosaur relatives. This is due to evolution. Living things evolve over very long periods of time, and their DNA changes. Even so, some birds do look like living dinosaurs. The southern cassowary is a large, heavy bird with a crest on its head. It cannot fly.

Southern cassowaries can be 6 feet (1.8 m) tall.

LIKE ALL BIRDS, HUMMINGBIRDS ARE RELATED TO DINOSAURS.

All modern birds descend from theropod dinosaurs. These were birdlike creatures with feathers. They ran on two feet. About 160 million years ago, smaller theropods appeared and began developing wings to fly. Could scientists use bird DNA to bring dinosaurs back to life? All birds today have very different DNA to the dinosaurs. So far, scientists have not been able to use it.

Clones

A clone is an exact copy of a living thing, even a cell. A clone has the same DNA as the original. A sheep named Dolly became the first mammal cloned from a single adult cell. Dolly was born in 1996. Scientists have also cloned mice, cows, and goats. Without any DNA samples to copy, cloning a dinosaur has been impossible.

AFTER DOLLY DIED, HER BODY WAS PRESERVED AND DISPLAYED IN A MUSEUM.

Fossilized hydrosaur eggs hold clues about how dinosaurs lived.

Signs of Life

In 2007 a fossilized baby mammoth was found in Siberia. The little mammoth had been preserved in the cold for about forty thousand years. Another baby mammoth was found in northern Canada in 2022. Scientists could not find any traces of DNA in the mammoths. In the 1980s paleontologists found a nest of fossilized hydrosaurus babies in Montana. About forty years later scientists found cells in the fossils. But so far they haven't found any DNA. As technology develops, and if there is any DNA there, scientists may find it.

Spotlight On:
Colossal Biosciences

Mammoths have been extinct for about four thousand years. In 2021 scientists found DNA samples in a tooth fossil. The tooth belonged to a mammoth in Siberia. Scientists at Colossal Biosciences are hoping to rebuild ancient mammoth DNA using information from mammoth fossils. Modern elephants are closely related to mammoths. Female elephants could be used to carry and give birth to baby mammoths.

A life-size model of a mammoth in front of a mammoth skeleton

Protecting the Future

Digging into the past can tell us a lot about the future. As Earth keeps warming up, how will it look different to Earth in the past? The findings in Greenland revealed that Arctic animals, such as reindeer and lemmings, survived in warmer places. They lived alongside animals known for surviving in warm climates, like mastodons. This information may give us clues about how creatures created through de-extinction could adapt to modern warmer habitats.

Reindeer typically live in cold places.

Bringing extinct animals back to life could be good and bad. While some animals may help to restore habitats, others could destroy them. Also, the animals may not survive on today's planet. Plant-eating dinosaurs did not eat grasses. Could they cope with these and other modern plants? Maybe they would adapt and eat too much. Meat-eating dinosaurs could destroy ecosystems and biodiversity by hunting too many animals.

Thinking about these and other questions can help people decide whether or not to try bringing back extinct animals. By considering the possible benefits against the drawbacks, we can create a safe world for all living things.

Cows adapted to survive on grass, but many other animals cannot digest it.

But What If We Did?

If dinosaurs are ever brought back to life, there will be many questions to answer. Where would they live? What about avian dinosaurs? Should they be allowed to stay wild and have the right to roam and fly freely? If dinosaurs could be tamed, would they live in zoos or could people keep them as pets? What would we feed them?

Glossary

avian: having to do with birds

biodiversity: a variety of living things in an environment

cell: smallest unit of all living things; humans have trillions of them

DNA: a part of cells that holds the instructions for how people, animals, and plants look and function

extinct: no longer existing

evolve: to develop and change over time

fossil: the preserved remains of a prehistoric plant or animal

organism: a living thing, such as an animal, plant, or germ

preserved: kept safe from ruin

reconstruct: to make or build again

resin: a sticky liquid found in some kinds of trees

Learn More

Britannica Kids: De-extinction
https://www.britannica.com/science/de-extinction

Humphrey, Natalie. *Dinosaur Fossils*. Scientific American Educational Publishing, 2025

Jackson, Tom. *T. Rex vs. Ankylosaurus: Prehistoric Showdown*. Lerner Publications, 2025

Lund, Nick. *Dinosaurs to Chickens*. Workman, 2024

Natural History Museum: Can We Bring Back Dinosaurs?
https://www.nhm.ac.uk/discover/could-scientists-bring-dinosaurs-back.html

Scholastic: Should We Bring Back Extinct Animals?
https://sn4.scholastic.com/pages/promotion/navigationlps/120621/should-we-bring-back-extinct-animals.html?language=english#On%20Level

Index

Photo Acknowledgments

Image credits: Muratart/Shutterstock, p. 5; benedek/iStock, p. 6; janiebros/istock, p. 7; Salajean/Dreamstime, p. 8; Bjoern Wylezich/Shutterstock, p. 9; Joe McUbed/iStock, p. 11; Vladimir Bolokh/Shutterstock, p. 12; Hugh K Telleria/Shutterstock, p.13; Kps1664/Shutterstock, p. 14; Lukasz Pawel Szczepanski/Shutterstock, p, 15; PARALAXIS/Shutterstock, p. 16; Duncan1890/iStock, p. 17; TomSmithDAF/Shutterstock, p. 19; Duncan1890/iStock, p. 20; Nikita G. Sidorov/Shutterstock, p. 21; DannyYe/Shutterstock, p. 22; Amine Chakour/Shutterstock, p. 23; Steph Couvrette/Shutterstock, p. 24; Jaroslav Moravcik/Shutterstock, p. 25; AKKHARAT JARUSILAWONG/Shutterstock, p. 26; ZADNANE Mohamed/Shutterstock, p. 27; Dmitry Pichugin/Shutterstock, p. 28.

Cover: Warpaint/Shutterstock.